LOVE, DEATH, HUMANISM

LOVE, DEATH, HUMANISM

Practical Philosophy in Verse

Dan Dana, PhD

Five Palms Press
Sarasota, Florida
dandana.us/fivepalms

Copyright © Dan Dana 2024

All text is authored by Dan Dana. No text was generated by AI. Photos and images not otherwise attributed were created by the author. Certain images were generated by AI, designated as "Image by AI (ImageFX)".

The number at the bottom of each haiku (/***) is a locator code indicating its place (1 to 419) in the sequence of compositions from September 2019 to present.

Contents

Preface vii
Introduction ix

Region 1. Love 1
Region 2. Death 41
Region 3. Humanism 83

Epilogue 107
Legacy 108
About Me 109
Acknowledgements 111
Other books 113

Preface

With Eyes Wide Open

you and I seek love
yearning to touch and be touched
to see and be seen

you and I will die
breaching our lone horizon
to be no longer

you and I wonder
who am I in the cosmos?
is this all there is?

we are both poets
seeking our own perfect words
where none can be found

you and I can share
this trek to oblivion
with eyes wide open

/395

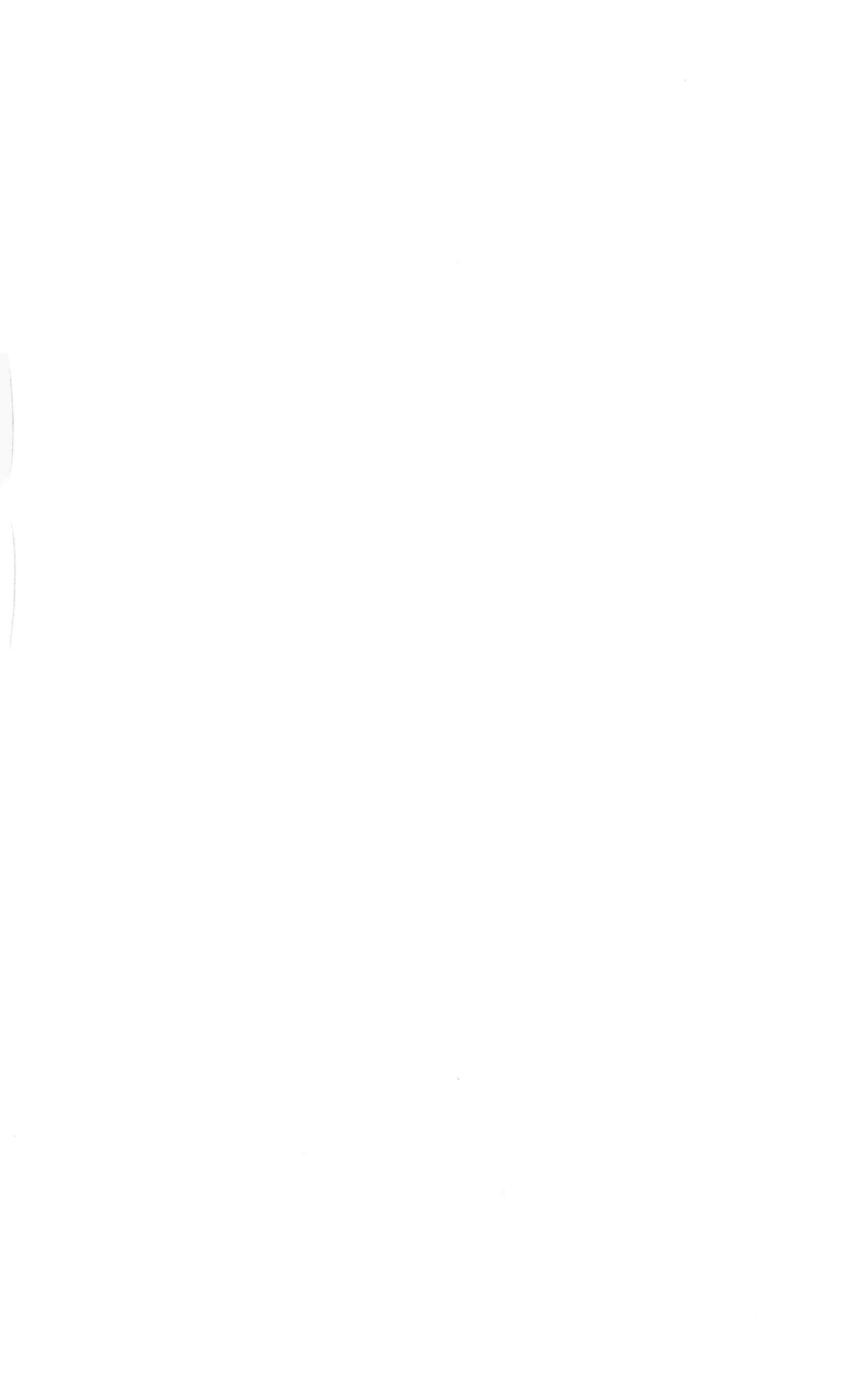

Introduction

Who does NOT seek love, or more abundant love — that glue that binds us to others, that makes us matter to each other, filling, albeit incompletely, the hole where loneliness otherwise abides?

Who does NOT accept, albeit with dread, the inescapable truth that they will die one day, that their trip will be over, that their personal horizon will be breached?

Who does NOT wonder, amid the hubbub of daily chores, what it all means, what is the big picture beyond local mundanity? Religion works for some. Others recognize the shortcomings of religious myths to explain the awesome reality of our miniscule moment within the unfathomably vast cosmos of infinite spacetime. What worldview best replaces the abandoned fairy tales of pre-science antiquity?

This curated collection of 103 haiku quintets contains evocative thought-snippets in each of these three regions of the mind.

The haiku quintet is an emergent poetic form, originated by the author and derived from the classical 17th Century Japanese style. In each, five 17-syllable haiku under an umbrella title comprise a topical theme. A photo or image illustrates and completes the finished piece, once described as "poetic impressionism by curious wordcraft."

Each of the three named sections—Love, Death, Humanism—contains pin-hole glimpses into these dimensions of human experience that curious minds have pondered for millennia. You are living a unique life, one that no one has lived before. It's now your turn. You're in charge. You love. You will die. What do you believe?

What about science? Several haiku contain reference to concepts in science, particularly cosmology, evolutionary biology, human paleontology, and psychology (the subject of my PhD and career). These mentions refer to settled, non-controversial findings or to prevailing professional theories in those disciplines.

They are not science fiction nor popular misconstructions of these fields. They represent objective reality as science has so far revealed it. I employ science here to substantiate the secular worldview that underlies my assertions of practical philosophy.

This book is not designed to be read front to back, although habit may impel you to do so. Your attention may be drawn more to one of its three headings than another. Within each, haiku are arranged in no strict order. Some verses may catch your interest, beckoning to be reread to dwell on its personal significance to you. Others you may find irrelevant to this moment in your life's journey.

Browse
Let your mind wander
Follow it there
Repeat

Region 1

Love

PLATO AND ARISTOTLE, astute observers of human nature, gave us language for that ubiquitous set of emotions we loosely call love. Some custom blend of their seven kinds of love (parsed elsewhere) defines our personal relationships today, 2400 years later. Human nature changes slowly.

In the following pages, I humbly employ my own life-partner and primary love object—from 1995 'til-death-do-us-part—as an exemplar. Her name is Susan. She is *my* ideal. *We* are the product of *our* relationship work. Your efforts to find, create, and cultivate love in your own life may produce a quite different result. Bits you encounter here, filtered through your own private lens, may help you find your way or confirm your own choices. If so, my task has been successful.

As you peruse these 29 haiku, Susan will be replaced in your mind's eye by your own love object(s)—perhaps your spouse or other partner, temporary or permanent, living or lost, same sex or other, monogamous or poly, happy or distressed, real or imagined. Let these haiku morph into your own unique living story.

Viewed through a wider lens than just romantic love, some haiku address other forms of affectionate attachment identified by our Greek philosophers. To adapt and repurpose a biblical quote, "Man does not love by romance alone."

DAN DANA

How to Make Love
(It's not what you think—it's better.)

no deep secret here
simple truth for keen partners
use this power tool:

pay close attention
mate's soft bids for connection
accept, don't reject

turn toward, not away
turn-aways kill trust, troth, love
turn-towards cement bond

listen when she* speaks
applaud her* career success
laugh at her* fun pun

meet kiss-hint with yours
subtle gestures flow both ways
turning toward makes love

* Feminine pronouns adopted as generic /69

LOVE, DEATH, HUMANISM

My Valentine

there's mojo in two
one eye's not enough, nor ear
one leg cannot stand

one heart's not enough
mine hardly beats without you
my self's other half

one plus one is three
in love's odd mathematics
our equation works

one half-life's too short
I have doubled-down on you
a winning wager

mi Valentina
you are twice the worth of me
with you, I am whole

Caricature by Sean Connor /185

Three Magic Words

practiced life partners
know well I-Love-You's effect
when sincerely voiced

triggers like response
reciprocity's reflex
ripens love's sweet taste

less known and practiced
three more magic power-words
when disputes erupt:

defenses push back
blame, fault, anger take the wheel
driving toward a ditch

harness that reflex
take high road to love's repair
asking, Tell-Me-More

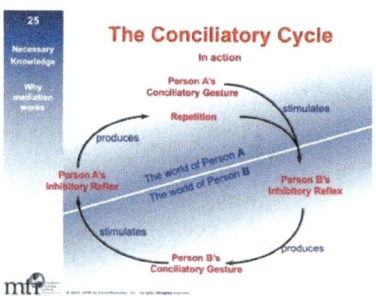

From mediation training course developed by Dan Dana
— www.mediationworks.com /144

LOVE, DEATH, HUMANISM

Puppies in a Box

it's often declared
among relationshipped folk:
"marriage is hard work"

not so, in our nest
I don't own you, nor you me
we are free to be

no promises bind
I choose you afresh each day
our freedom's unchained

kindnesses gifted
each in debt to the other
balance sheets in rhyme

primal friendship's root
loving's simple sauce known by
puppies in a box

Image by AI (ImageFX) /18

DAN DANA

My Schizoid Compromise*

how close do I come,
daring to let you see me
—<u>real</u> me, warts and all?

and, how far away
do I stay hidden from you,
safe from your arrows?

writing these haiku,
now shared on the world wide web,
reveals my answer

browsing these secrets,
you may peer into my core
through frosted windows

I'm only human,
managing my boundaries,
just like you, my friend

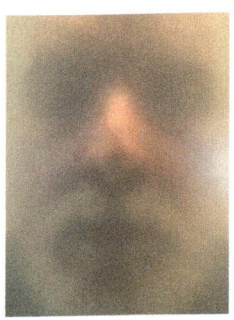

* A term from object relations theory coined by psychoanalyst Melanie Klein /293

LOVE, DEATH, HUMANISM

Hear The Other Side

in comfy silos
we hear only our echoes
muting others' sides

our firm opinions
rest on facts *we* choose to hear
not heard by *your* side

we do not convict
people we accuse of crimes
'til we hear their side

when trapped in conflict
there is only one escape:
hear the other's side

from ancient wisdom:
*audi alteram partem**
"hear the other side"

* A Latin phrase originating in Greek drama, a maxim in English law, a truism in mediation, a precondition for love

Speakers' Corner, Hyde Park, London /327

Simple Magic*

stay in dialog,
resist tug to walk away
or to power-play

patience wins the war,
raise risk's scared but daring head
above the foxhole

trust peace's process
as Mother Apology,
bravely lifts her veil

me-against-you fades,
us-against-it emerges,
"we" supersedes "I"

both science and art,
mediation's a life-skill
—it's simple magic

* The original working title of *Managing Differences* /121

LOVE, DEATH, HUMANISM

Economics of Love

clean underwear, socks
mysteriously appear
in dresser drawers

Sunday brunch specials
just magically show up
at my table place

I'm deeply in debt
my remittances fall short
of the balance due

she accepts payment
in curious currencies
from my bank's account

exchange rates vary
but each thinks we are winning
—rich beyond measure

/163

Transactional Love

fairness your focus?
getting less than you're giving?
wrong frame for true love!

keep score: self-defeat
counting your cash ensures loss
winning is losing

transactional love?
oxymoron, can't compute
quid pro quo shorts both

one plus one is ten
yielding love's rich abundance
let it multiply

not-to-win's the goal
no-secrets is the secret
surrender control

/56

LOVE, DEATH, HUMANISM

Reciprocity

that glue that joins us:
reciprocity's soft nudge,
your kind act's applause

"I hear you, my friend
I accept your outstretched hand
I'm here in your world"

but in reply's void,
the sound of one hand clapping,
what am I to hear?

no answer ... I wait ...
nature abhors a vacuum*
assumptions rush in

you and I respond,
we accept the outstretched hand,
we're here in our world

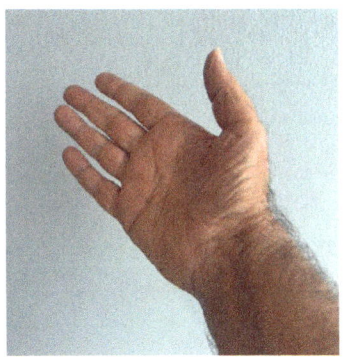

* A concept attributed to Aristotle /358

— 11 —

Decrypting Woman

countless blunderings
litter my long winding path
to this latter day

decades of missed cues
my garbled ear could not hear
my blurred eye couldn't see

his-and-her desires
vulnerabilities glimpsed
in funhouse mirrors

coded messages
modestly sought undressing
sometimes urgently

fumbling for access
hacking your encryption key
guessing your password

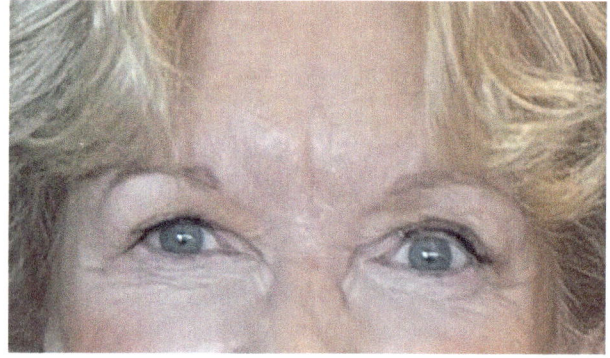

/201

Femininity

your sniffable neck
fragrant female pheromones
my breakfast bouquet

your nuclear touch
electrons desire protons
charged ions snuggle

male seeking female
so glad you reciprocate
this force of nature

primal energy
exquisite polarity
magnetic allure

could I resist your
lovely feminine power?
probably, … but why?

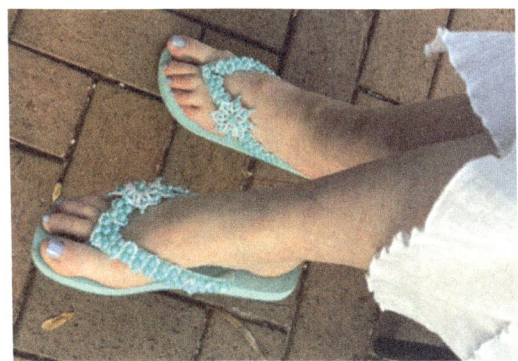

/362

DAN DANA

Fixer-Upper

it seems I'm due for
some repairs and improvements
I had not noticed

nose hair needs trimming
comfy draw-string shorts are stained
… among more eyesores

I live in her nest
needing frequent attention
—a fixer-upper

is she tending to
her investment property
that's losing value?

or is she simply
tending to my self-neglect
because she loves me?

/357

Angel on Earth

no spirit-elf myth
if angels on earth there be
I know one quite well:

foresees others' wants
nurse-caregiver at her core
off-scale mindfulness

nurtures by nature
advocate for those in need
champ of voice-and-choice

tenacious fixer
restores sundered children with
mama-bear fierceness

makes our house a home
kindest person ever known
I kiss her nightly

The angel (1953) /50

LOVE, DEATH, HUMANISM

A Coding Error

she said what she meant
in well-chosen word-symbols
perfectly clearly

he heard what he chose
"I know her intent," he thought
"I read her script"

he replied with care
in same language (so it seemed)
"now we're clear," he judged

but something went wrong
unseen filters warped our view?
or coding error?

neither of us knew:
what I heard's not what you meant
'round and 'round and 'round

/161

LOVE, DEATH, HUMANISM

Bon Voyage

we're a cruising team
crossing fierce Pandemic Sea*
each other's first mate

rising every morn
navigating through each day
'til our goodnight kiss

we share the tiller
steering clear of rocky shoals
and far shore's dark reef

yon fog-shrouded coast
who can know this journey's end?
we bid bon voyage

co-traveling friend
love's expedition partner
sailing toward life's dusk

* Composed during COVID-19 pandemic (2020) /152

DAN DANA

Kissing Quandary

so snug on the couch
blanket tucked under your chin
blonde wisps frame your face

your afternoon nap
this precious at-home Sunday,
you've been working hard

sweet love swells my heart,
we're two puppies in a box
sharing life's comforts

might I sneak a kiss
on your cheek, but not wake you?
my lips want your warmth

no, you need this rest
you would lift your sleepy head
to greet my sly kiss

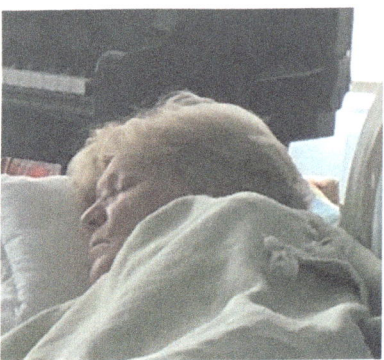

Photo taken from my desk while writing this haiku /266

LOVE, DEATH, HUMANISM

Haiku Disruptor

early morning spoon
my arm wraps your hand-cupped flesh
no sound but breathing

your dawn-glinted hair
our warm body-melt sandwich
puppies in a box

like aching beauty
of fading, dying sunset
permanence denied

sleep-washed brain cells stir
this perfect moment disturbed
words disrupt my peace

restless, twitching mind
wrests me from snug partnered bliss
to write this haiku

/165

DAN DANA

Where Is Your Beauty?

out there or in here?
where lies your beauty's lodestar?
in you or in me?

my admiring eye
quaffs your yummy countenance,
quenching my heart's thirst

our rich alchemy,
a master chef's concoction
so sweet to my taste

lovers' featured asset,
poets' raw material
since dawn of love's time

words cannot capture
this art we draw together
on love's shared canvas

At former home of Elizabeth Taylor, Puerto Vallarta /355

LOVE, DEATH, HUMANISM

Statement of Purpose

on our balcony
on Calle Jacaranda
twelve hard years ago

your wailing grief surged
from depths only mothers know
—I would be your rock

words rose from my soul,
you deserve all I can give,
my unfailing love:

*"My life has no higher purpose
than to contribute to the
quality of your life"**

this broken haiku
hopes to repair your trauma
in some small measure

* This 15-word *Statement of Purpose* found voice on the day Susan received news of her son's unsurvivable cancer in Puerto Vallarta, Mexico, 2010. He died in 2015. /340

DAN DANA

Resilience

you are kind, thoughtful,
and generous to a fault
you are an angel

strangers who stumble
into your warm sunshine are
stunned by your goodness

we who know you best
who return your love with love
are the lucky ones

but those who squander,
who trample your sweet kindness
discard a treasure

your softness is strength
you can rally from setback
you're resilient

Susan began learning piano at age 70 /326

LOVE, DEATH, HUMANISM

Skin Therapy

grief overwhelms you
no good answers to be found
no words sooth your pain

can nothing be done?
am I helpless to help you?
must you cope alone?

skin therapy heals
we lie together naked
skin-to-skin-to-skin

mine feeds yours feeds mine
you absorb love through your pores
no talk, no action

therapeutic balm
of pure animal essence
the best medicine

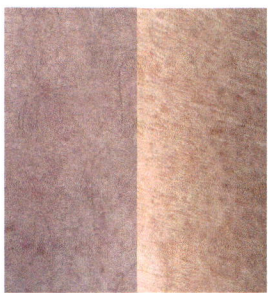

Dan(l) – Susan(r)
Patches of skin that often touch each other /292

DAN DANA

She's Not Done Yet

morning's alarm sounds
wake me at eight, you had asked
"I am not done yet"

did you finish the
audiobook on your walk?
"I am not done yet"

bacon on your plate,
which I eye with interest
"I am not done yet"

birthdays piling up,
stack getting fretfully high
"I am not done yet"

my idle question,
do you still love me, my Dear?
"I am not done yet"

/119

LOVE, DEATH, HUMANISM

How to Choose a Spouse

answer four questions,
find your shared lives fulfilling,
or a pail of tears:

can we be best friends?
mutual respect, liking,
trust in guilelessness

does sex work for us?
we are natural creatures
beneath cosmetics

are our wants in sync?
lifestyle preferences play
in the same ballpark

can we talk it out?
we can find common ground
for a path forward

July 1, 2000 /344

— 25 —

Relationship Black Holes

I bid for contact
you star in my universe
I care about you

I send a quantum
bundle of loving wattage
checking our tether

like cosmic namesake
energy goes in, none out
from dark closed system

best keep my distance?
where's your event horizon,
your heart's boundary?

Susan? no such doubt
your bright star lights my lifespace
our gravities meld

Image: Scientific American /98

The Bridge Between

bound by life itself
we two islands lie conjoined
tied by shared genome

uneven traffic
pulses sent, trickle returns
from bloodline's black hole

our clan's push-and-pull
generation gap cleaves us
cohorts entreat us

both sides left forlorn
I know what we've lost, do you?
fog will rise, in time

this span shall not fail
force of will and love prevail
the bridge between stands

/63

DAN DANA

Existential Borderland

we touch, I feel you
separated by our skins
we're near, but not one

we meet, I see you
separated by our masks
we're near, but not one

we talk, I hear you
separated by our words
we're near, but not one

we care, we share love
separated by our selves
we're near, but not one

we're close, but alone
a borderland lies between
no yoke can meld us

/213

An Old Flame

she reached across miles
decades and careers in time's dust
an email surprise

adjusting life-plans
rescripted in middle age
in personals ad

we explored ourselves
with witty conversation
warming our brief space

our journeys diverged
seemed lost to forgotten days
then … my inbox rang

how are you, old friend?
I want to learn about you
and about myself

MSR /92

The Wrong Susan

"good morning, Susan,
I've landed in Miami"
she paused, seemed confused

overnight flight's daze
mixed up my reminder notes,
"sorry, my mistake"

I owed her a call
back home, I apologized
I blew it, I thought

not the jealous type
one of her fine qualities
partner-type, for me

retired together
in our condo by the bay
she's the right Susan

/243

LOVE, DEATH, HUMANISM

Finding Her

like ripening fruit
he was growing more ready
to re-pair his life

he'd relived a time
he had never lived before
only imagined

wiser choice, this time
he had learned the recipe
of love's secret sauce

armed with his treatise*
he sallied Cupid's broad plain
vision in focus

his arrow struck gold
two puppies snug in our box
'til death we'll remain

Compatibility Factors (unpublished) /243

Song for Susan

dear co-traveler,
this path we chose together
hand in hand we go

your innate wisdom
guiding me and growing me
showing me myself

our trust seals our bond
no dark suspicions intrude
e duo unum

simple humanism
no supernatural myths
we believe in us

onward 'til our end
living day by precious day
my best friend, my love

/5

LOVE, DEATH, HUMANISM

The Real Lesson

I fancied myself
a fast runner, at age nine
could I beat my mom?

she took my challenge
to the far mulberry tree
she easily won

I was deflated
she hugged me with love and grace
I learned a lesson:

in whatever field
underestimate my mom
at your own peril

for years thereafter
she was sorry for winning
—love's the real lesson

My mom (1918-2009) displaying another of her remarkable talents at age 89, April 2008 /247

DAN DANA

My Dad at 150

on this Father's Day
we're getting up there in years,
you and I, Old Man

my mythic totem,
you are who I've strived to be
in fatherless dreams

dwindling few of us
recall your twinkling blue eyes
as thoughts stirred your mind

when I reach your years
who'll recall my twinkling eyes?
some aging poet?

meanwhile, life goes on,
I'm busy living each day,
just as you were, Dad

J. W. Dana (1874-1955), photo circa 1925 /33

LOVE. DEATH. HUMANISM

Sibling Love

we shared Mom and Dad
our DNA overlaps
joined at the genome

as kids we played nice
decades passed, we found our mates
our grandchildren grow

our journeys diverged
miles stretch between our homes
and our worldviews

love takes sundry forms
not mates nor just friends are we
nor offspring most dear

lifelong sibling bond
unlike any other tie
Sis, Bub, I love you

Dan – Deana – Jon (2019) /24

Inexpressible

in one precious frame,
the three women I love most,
tracing my heart's joy

this spindly haiku
struggles to carry the freight
of love's sundry forms

too few syllables,
my thin thesaurus falls short
surely there's a way!

for want of language,
all who burst with love's heartbeat
wear this poet's shoes

inexpressible
in words known to humankind
d'ya know what I mean?

Wife – Granddaughter – Daughter (2021) /214

LOVE, DEATH, HUMANISM

Love's Origin Story

newborn needs its mom
in sync, mom needs her newborn
—oxytocin floods

moms' love of babies
spans cultures, species, eons,
—the primeval bond

fruits of her womb count
ten thousand generations,
life's unbroken chain

birthing and nursing,
she would kill to protect them
by primal instinct

the girl fell in thrall,
igniting her life's passion
—babies rule the world

Personal collection of Susan, a mother-baby nurse

DAN DANA

Newborn

welcome to the world
held in loving arms and hearts
you're one lucky kid

though you can't yet know
your keen senses surely feel
that love swaddles you

what wonders await
what sights your wide eyes will see
what far lands you'll know

you'll climb life's mountains
and plumb its valleys' dark depths
learning as you go

those who gave you life
love you just for who you are
not for what you'll do

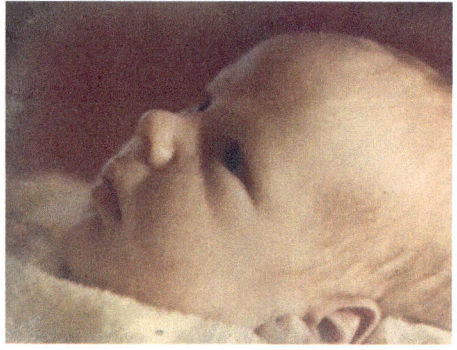

Tyghe (1977-2015) /218

LOVE, DEATH, HUMANISM

In Mommy's Eyes

you are my whole world
you have no name but Mommy
you and I are one

I glow in your eyes
no border separates us
I'm still inside you

your face delights me
I see me in your eyes' gleam
your smile is my joy

not-me is just you
I want nothing else but you
you give me myself

now is eternal
here is only you and me
love is all there is

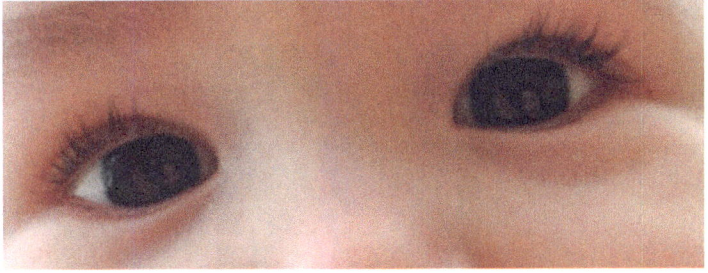

In object relations theory, ego begins to form from the moment of birth when the newborn attempts to relate to the world. Mother's breast, then face, are the first external objects to be known. Photo credit: Sara Scott. /223

My Relief Generation

Dedication of my memoir, *A Life Mostly Lived*

nearing the hand-off
of my lap with the baton
your turn has begun

our story's passed on
distant past to far future
one life at a time

shrouded in folklore
memory's fleeting half-life
decays to fragments

save this slim box of
Papi's memory snippets
for your relievers

as future unfurls
preserve your lap's key moments
—the relay goes on

Seamus and Claribel (2006) / 321

Region 2

Death

The idea of death becomes an ever more powerful attractor the closer it appears on the uncertain horizon, like a magnet as it nears the opposite pole. I'm pushing eighty. I'm drawn in like a moth to flame, watching warily as I circle its vortex.

This portion of the book contains forty haiku quintets. None are morbid or gruesome. I hope to die peacefully and lucidly. I do not fear actually being dead. Holding an atheistic, non-spiritual worldview, I anticipate no afterlife. I behold in wonder the stark reality before me, that I will die and the world will go on, just as I have gone on after the deaths of my parents, and humanity has gone on for millions of generations of ancient and pre-human ancestors who each died. And, in some post-human sentient form, we will go on until life's final extinction some five billion years hence as the expanding sun vaporizes our planet. In choosing to live, such is our bargain with fate.

I offer these verses hoping that you, dear mortal reader, may find inspiration, joy in living your awesome finite existence, and wise acceptance of its end.

My Obituary
(An early draft)

migrant of the mind
who could not resist asking,
"what's life's big picture?"

avid collector
of worldly experience,
his lifelong hobby

career was a drill
to probe psyche's precious gems,
he dared to dig deep

dismantler of myths,
sought to fathom our true place
in this vast cosmos

educator strove
to leave world a smarter place,
now returned to dust

Dan Dana
9/23/1945—?/?/20??
Educator – Mediator – Poet
/413

LOVE, DEATH, HUMANISM

LUCKY LIFE
1945 – 20??

born at World War's end,
lived 'til democracy died(?)*
lifespan's perfect plan

escaped ancients' pain,
far surpassed royals' comforts,
skipped predators' lunch

goods and services,
luxuries beyond belief
with middle class means

great while it lasted,
lucky place and lucky time,
I'm a lucky schmuck

fortunes turning dark
as human story unfurls,
I mourn future's child

* Ominous clouds appear on America's political horizon at the time of this writing (August 2024)

Image by AI (ImageFX): There but for fate went I. /402

— 43 —

DAN DANA

LEGACIES DIE TOO

death's specter nears,
I've kicked my can down the road
two generations

years or decades more?
I may live another day,
but brute fact remains:

my checklist of done-that's,
once carefully curated,
must fade from time's plan

vain fantasies dwell
in mortals' void afterlife,
memoir's futile myth

legacies die, too,
I sigh in meek surrender
—'til my next haiku

Cover of volume II of my memoir (scheduled 2025) /384

LOVE, DEATH, HUMANISM

Being Dead*

no darkness, no light
nothing at all, forever
no past, no future

time after I die
will not pass—same timelessness
as before my birth

here will not be there
who I was will be no more
no me, no not-me

no regret, no loss
no loneliness, no sadness
no fear, no gladness

no pain, no pleasure
no now, no then, no being
—pure nothingness reigns

* This description becomes obvious once religion (supernaturalism) is discarded. /411

My Deathbed

I'll die in this bed
if my life ends as I hope,
a calm, peaceful death

days are not numbered,
circumstances not yet known,
blind corners remain

my legacy's cast:
books* known to all I have loved,
read by all who care

when pain exceeds joy,
may no law trespass this right:
my death is my choice

in life-partner pact,
we may take this road as one,
love shared to its end

* Memoir, *A Life Mostly Lived,* and other volumes /370

LOVE, DEATH, HUMANISM

My Sell-by Date

when will I have reached
memory's slippery slope?
are there clear signposts?

point of no return,
death's door of choice shuttered tight,
exit's key is lost

as sell-by date nears
or if hers precedes my own,
we may share the plunge

I forget friends' names,
new games' rules befuddle me,
I repeat myself,

I like "the old way,"
I reveal more than I should,
as in this haiku

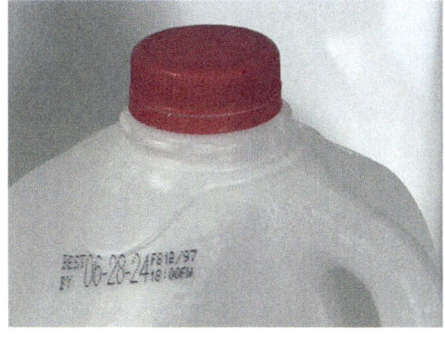

/377

DAN DANA

The Crime of Killing Time

quarantine fillers*
empty tasks devoid of worth
staving off boredom

life's stark finitude
nonrenewable resource
spent one day per day

youth's bottomless cup
unconcerned by careless spills
blinded by plenty

elders' clearer sight
murky depth comes into view
we savor each drop

tilting once-full cup
heeding crime of killing time
I sip slowly now

* Composed during COVID-19 pandemic quarantine (2020) /160

LOVE, DEATH, HUMANISM

Slippery Slope

on tongue's tender tip
names of known people and things
stubbornly resist

my urgent summons
in daily conversations
at senior moments

friends say, "yeah, me too"
but their words seem to appear
when called to duty!

how did your brains work,
oh pioneer ancestors,
as age beset you?

were you forgetful?
did you sense, with worried mind,
that slippery slope?

/408

How Is Life Good?

bomb-crushed Gazans scream
hostages wail for release
last hope fades to black

Ukrainians die
like Putin's captured conscripts
blending blood with mud

hordes pound border wall
fleeing homelands' misery
so near, door slams shut

in this pain-drenched world
some victims grace our news screens,
but most never do

please tell me again,
believers in loving gods,
just how is life good?

Ground zero, Hiroshima, Japan (2003) /405

LOVE, DEATH, HUMANISM

Alzheimer's Dream

we were traveling
got separated somehow
I asked directions

but took a wrong turn
forgot where he said to go
I'm getting worried

I am so confused
this place is unfamiliar
I can't find my phone

where could she have gone?
I hope she's looking for me
I want to be home

suddenly, I wake,
relieved it was just a dream,
but seemed so damned real

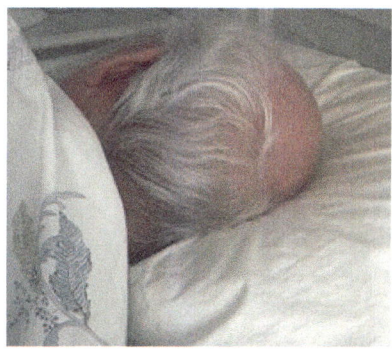

/382

Cyborg

my heart skips some beats,
not in a romantic way,
as aging proceeds

born nearly perfect,
but years take their cruel toll
—it's time for repairs

my Linq snitched on me,
told my cardiologist
I need more implants

stuffed with devices,
my body's just partly mine
—I'm a cyborg now

my new prognosis:
I may now live forever!
—thanks, Dr Eckart

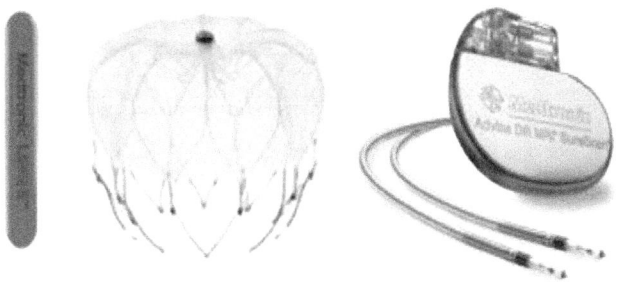

Parts of the new me (l-r): Linq cardiac monitor, Watchman stroke prevention device, pacemaker /363

LOVE, DEATH, HUMANISM

THE MOST MORAL CHOICE

most living things die
by being eaten alive
by a predator

"selfish genes" don't care
about our personal throes,
only our species

pain evolved to serve
the survival of our breed
at each one's expense

what is life's virtue
if its price is agony
of sentient beings?

our most moral choice:
bring no new life to the world,
prevent suffering

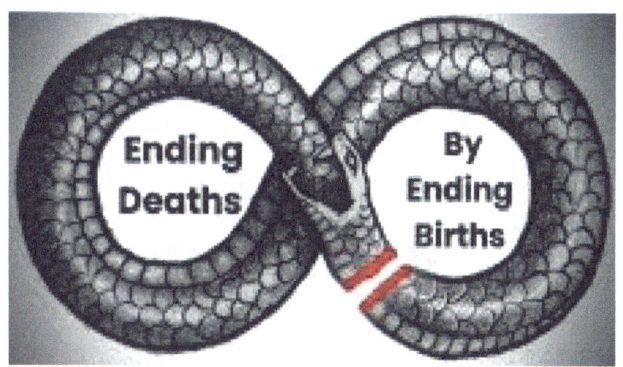

Image: Tamil Antinatalism /351

DAN DANA

Descendancy

I fathered one child,
she birthed two more lovely lives
—when will my line end?

unless we die off,
my descendants may witness
planet's final days

my heirs will suffer
Earth's certain calamities
through millennia

untold extinctions
will spawn subspecies of us
—life will find a way

countless known unknowns
await the hapless creatures
I caused to exist

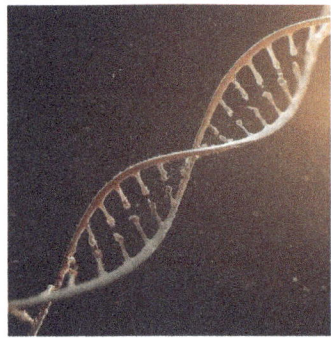

Image by AI (ImageFX) /349

Glidepath

descending apace
no refueling allowed
no airport's ahead

at my window seat
between clouds of denial
I glimpse rising ground

writing haiku is
free inflight entertainment
a fun distraction

if life is well planned
remaining time and money
end on the same day

a painless crash, I hope
enjoy the rest of this trip
—a terminal flight

/335

Have I Made a Difference?

most mortals hope to
leave the world a better place
as their exit nears

my career's true north
was teaching peacemaking skills
for both work and home

I often wonder
where and when those talking tools
made a difference:

in lands I've not seen?
in languages I don't speak?
in lives not yet lived?

now, I write haiku
a frivolous exercise,
but may help someone?

Teaching conflict resolution at Univ of Hartford, 1979 /311

LOVE, DEATH, HUMANISM

A Decision Deferred

failing socially
failing academically
failing with women

my future looked bleak
happiness felt beyond reach
I despaired of hope

a flash of insight
one day brightened my dark sky
—I could end my life!

I'd found a way out
of my doom's dreary prison
I was free to choose!

so ... do it today?
there's no rush, I decided
—and there still isn't

Setting: Freshman year, University of Missouri (1963-64) Photo: Return visit to campus with Susan (2019) /274

DAN DANA

I Forgot to Ask

Grandpa, where were you
when the First World War broke out?
I forgot to ask

Grandma, tell me tales
about my great-grandmother
I forgot to ask

Dad, how did you choose
your career, and your first wife?
I forgot to ask

Mom, what did you like
about Dad when you first met?
I forgot to ask

kids, I'm getting old
anything you'd like to know?
don't forget to ask

My mom on her final birthday (2008) /228

LOVE, DEATH, HUMANISM

My Bucket List

yup, been there, done that
I have sailed Earth's seven seas
I've climbed Rockies' peaks

untold adventures
stored in my memory bank
life's been great ... still is

old age marches forth
contentment replaces thrill
pleasure's in small things

gazing on the bay
admiring other men's boats
glad they are not mine

to live happily
doing bits of good each day
—that's my bucket list

/224

DAN DANA

Five Seconds Left to Live

five seconds to live:
asleep, the usual dreams
not a care, all's well

four seconds to live:
I'm falling! … is this a dream?
panic jolts slumber

three seconds to live:
deafening roar, chaos whelms
what is happening?

two seconds to live:
NO! this can't be real! STOP! HELP!
is this how I die?

one second to live:
final breath crushed from my chest
death's abyss … the end

Condo collapse, Surfside, Florida, 24 July 2021, 1:30 a.m. Photo: CNN /216

LOVE, DEATH, HUMANISM

Only a Mother Can Know

her soul-crushing loss
secreted behind a veil
of smiling good cheer

grief's smothering shroud
cloaks her tomb of living death
gladness can't enter

but few know her pain
mothers' tear-drenched lost-child club
woe to those who join

pin-hole view each way:
our sweet love and lucky life;
her dark dismal cave

despair's icy grip
can't endure but can't move on
none but moms can know

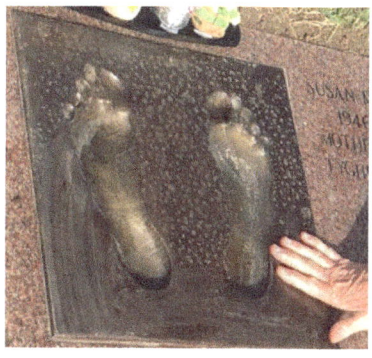

Her son's foot molds in bronze (2016)   /189

Final Moments

Covid's victim horde*
enduring final moments
thoughts ebbing, alone

nurse's tear-wet face
ventilator's steady beat
light fading to black

I wish you comfort
know your life was not in vain
your good deeds remain

yielding to abyss
at eternal Nothing's door
pain is near its end

so, this is death, at last?
being loved by those you've loved
goodbye to the world

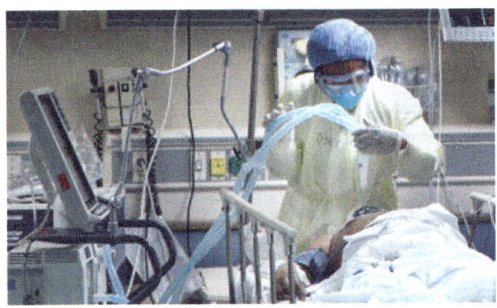

* Over 7,000,000 people have died of COVID-19 worldwide as of June 2024 (CNN and other sources) /166

On Nihilism: 1

the world is so big
the universe is so vast
I am so tiny

time is infinite
history spans forever
my life is so short

leaders fail their task
I see, care, but cannot do
I am powerless

I am but a drop
in the Sea of Existence,
insignificant

but I can watch, awed,
in the company of friends
'til my movie ends

Photo: Technology /387

On Nihilism: 2

I will write haiku,
I'll vote, pay tax, obey laws,
be kind to others

I cannot prevent
evil despots' senseless wars,
children's suffering

few will know I lived
when my dust returns to dust
and memories fade

'til then, here I am
observing my one moment,
awed that I exist

I'll accept, not fight,
surrender my will to fate,
be. here. now. in peace

The haikuist in his moment /158

LOVE, DEATH, HUMANISM

Along for the Ride

I'm a spectator
of world's unfolding drama
one unit of life

I'm not at the wheel
just a wide-eyed passenger
hurtling through spacetime

on Earth's fragile skin
voyaging the vast unknown
along for the ride

immersed in deep awe
of this accidental trip
as long as it lasts

I'll binge on life's feast
with gratitude for blind luck
'til my final bite

Our home-hatched chick out for a ride, much like me /151

— 65 —

Unspent Wealth

one lifetime's gems
cast off as trifling pebbles
of dubious worth

my world-wise elders
went to their final abyss,
their wealth left behind

young ones stay busy
tending to urgent matters,
as did I, back then

wishing I knew then
one ounce of what I now know
of life's rare riches

here, take this flotsam,
this memoir of unspent wealth,
my left-behind gems

Standing at exact site of my father's 1874 pioneer cabin birthplace in Humboldt, Kansas, located in 2023   /137

LOVE, DEATH, HUMANISM

Racing Against Time

this healthy old man
should survive Covid's bad bug,
but still, there's a chance

this haiku e-book
may be my life's legacy,
if finished in time

we social-distance,
we facemask responsibly,
our friend pool is small

rushing to complete,
and forward to publisher,
before I'm struck dead

Florida hotspot's
not a safe place to hide while
racing against time

Selfie while composing this haiku, 28 July 2020 /123

Dylan Thomas and Me

quoth the young poet:
"rage, rage against the dying
of the light"—or not?

myself, I think not
—I'll marvel in that moment,
what a trip I've had!

grateful for my Now,
thinking thoughts about this thought,
cosmos' gift of mind

as this one-way ends,
savoring final moments,
drifting into void,

I intend to go
"gentle into that good night"
I was here—that's all*

*If I had faced death at age 39, I, too, may have raged. Dylan Thomas (1914-1953) /116

LOVE, DEATH, HUMANISM

Jim's Gift

he reached out to me,
final-exit day nearing,
to bid me farewell

I admire him so,
foresaw slippery slope's brink
with clear-eyed courage

choice was his to make,
appraised remaining time's worth,
as is Reason's way

his life amply lived,
left this world a better place,
his friends enriched

Jim's last gift to me:
clearer view of road ahead
—thank you, my wise friend

Inspired by Jim C. Image by AI (ImageFX) /100

DAN DANA

Life's a Movie

we're in this wild show,
director's chair sits vacant,
stage feels oddly real

comic bits bring laughs,
some so scary I can't watch,
tragic scenes bring tears

take a seat, my friend
relax, it's not about us,
let's watch together

que será, será
whatever will be, will be
will be fun to see

grim spoiler alert:
finale is known: The End
meanwhile, share popcorn

Image by AI (ImageFX) /70

LOVE, DEATH, HUMANISM

Death's Silver Lining

a child's death grieves us,
loved ones left to mourn their loss,
a young life cut short

thin silver lining:
no progeny will follow,
countless lives unlived,

myriad deaths spared,
war, misery, torment, fear
in longtermism's view

would joy outweigh pain?
antinatalists question:
better not to live?

we fortunate few
know but this cloudless moment
in life's roiling storm

/61

DAN DANA

Just You and Me

for nine loving months
before birthing, sharing you
with the waiting world
                    it was just you and me

I nursed you to life,
I fiercely held you to me,
I protected you

now you're gone, so gone,
lost to my sore, sobbing soul,
no soft skin to sooth

none knew you like me,
none loved how I loved you,
no one cared like me

my mother-love aches,
you remain inside me still,
a hole in my heart
                    again, it's just you and me

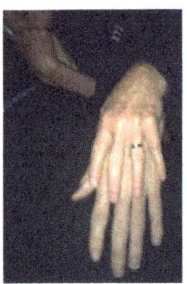

Mother and son shortly before his death (2015)   /47

Antinatalist Ethics

we seldom ask: why
life's bowl of tasty cherries
enjoyed by so few?

pain trumps pleasure on
history's skewed balance sheet,
ask evil's victims

animal cousins
suffer death by predator,
or meat factory

evolution's tool:
pain serves genome's goal, not ours,
in life's lethal game

ethicists debate,
consensus is not truth's proof,
paradigms can shift

Image: Antinatalism International /35

Package Deal

I'm nearly eighty
can't recall your name, dang it!
one of aging's peeves

ambition's kaput
energy tank's running low
that's how I roll, friends

trade brains with teen boy?
only if I keep wisdom
from life's lessons learned

libido? don't ask
testosterone? good riddance!
I'll keep these old bones

body's loss: mind's gain
can't have one without other
it's a package deal

/10

LOVE, DEATH, HUMANISM

When I Die

as life leaves this eye,
what will I say to the world
at final exit?

as Mother Cosmos
retrieves borrowed molecules:
"deep thanks for the loan!"

awesome luck at birth
fate's whim smiled kindly on me,
vastly more than most

I'll live 'til I don't,
the day not yet known to me,
but I choose to choose

my life, not others'
until it slips from my grasp,
it's mine to decide

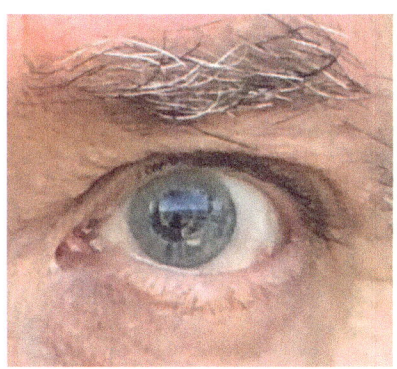

Selfie /9

Survival

beaucoup close calls in
this bumpy eighty-year romp,
tons of lucky breaks:

motorcycle crash:
Honduran priests saved my butt,
kept souvenir scars

Vietnam antics:
hazy memories survive,
Bronze Star for ganja

now safely cocooned
in Sarasota treehouse
for the duration

few dangers ahead
except the one that kills me
… patiently waiting

Selfie /103

LOVE, DEATH, HUMANISM

A Whimsy of Fate

as a kid, I thought
my life would last forever,
death hid behind Now

grown, in the abstract,
I understood I must die,
but distant specter

now nearing eighty,
as my life's been mostly lived,
death's shroud is slipping

my mom, at ninety,
murmured "it went by so fast!"
she died the next day

on the cosmic scale
my scant existence is but
a whimsy of fate

Ultra Deep Field by NASA's Webb Telescope. Most dots are one of the two trillion galaxies in the observable universe, up to 13.2 billion lightyears away in spacetime. Our Milky Way galaxy contains 400 billion stars. Our sun is one ordinary star. Scale is beyond comprehension. /342

DAN DANA

Rest In Peace

closer to life's end
than to its brash beginning,
I watch curtains close

at an odd remove,
as from a far mountaintop
through rose-colored lens

but for you young ones
and those zillions yet to live,
my bleeding heart grieves

what will beset you?
what torment will you endure?
what fate will snare you?

meanwhile, life is good
I've lived in charmed time and place
I'm resting in peace

/107

LOVE, DEATH, HUMANISM

My Dad's Earthly Afterlife

smoking was not blamed,
no one knew it was cancer
that was killing him

coughing up dark blood
he got sick in mid-winter,
did he see his fate?

I am his youngest,
us kids stayed with Grandmother
to shield us, I s'pose

last time I saw him,
snaked tubes in oxygen tent,
he was not moving

and then he was gone …
glimpsed in wistful, wishful dreams
he still breathes in me

J. W. Dana and family (1952) /272

Misplaced Grief

when I die, I'll cease,
no missed bucket-list regrets,
just pure nothingness

I'm not who will grieve,
you may mourn your loss of me,
a missed kith or kin

culture's vain last rite,
my funeral's not for me,
I will not be there

celebrate my life,
it's been one hell of a ride
—then, get on with yours

I'll drink life's last drop,
but if the end's too bitter,
please pass the hemlock

/220

LOVE, DEATH, HUMANISM

My Afterlife

my molecules may
join other Earthly life-forms:
mouse, bird, fish, worm, tree

as dad, my genes will
walk, talk, think, feel, reproduce
through offspring's tenure

my atoms will roam
worldwide 'til Earth's final gasp
five billion years hence

Sun's sons will explode:
generations of star-stuff,
my galactic tour

as teacher-writer,
some remnants may last awhile
—perhaps this haiku?

/169

Region 3

Humanism

<u>Humanism</u>: A secular worldview whose central concern is the wellbeing of people and other sentient animals. Humanists regard scientific empiricism as the only way to achieve knowledge of objective reality, eschewing religion and other supernaturalistic beliefs.

I have not always been an atheist. Reared on a family farm in the Protestant Christian milieu of the American Midwest, I absorbed the cultural and religious dogma of my community. I had never knowingly met an atheist.

In childhood, as now, I was drawn to existential wonderings about the Big Questions: Who am I? Why am I here? When will I die? What happened before and what comes next? The answers imparted weekly by our country preacher failed to quiet my persistent questioning.

At about age fifteen I met Gary, the visiting teenage grandson of rural neighbors, who gave me a small book by British philosopher Bertrand Russell. Gary was my first atheist. As dogma's cataracts peeled away, I began to see fresh light. Russell's clear-eyed rationality upended the blind faith I had inherited.

Leaving the farm for college and the wider world, I was exposed to scientific empiricism—rational inquiry using factual evidence—as an alternative means of knowing. I had thus found a better way to answer my questions than through the muddle of divine revelation and religious authority.

These pages contain 22 poetic glimpses into the secular-humanist worldview that replaced the supernaturalism of my childhood faith. See my 2014 book *The Reason Revolution: Atheism, Secular Humanism, and the Collapse of Religion* for a concise, non-poetic narrative.

I recognize that not every reader will concur with my non-theistic, non-supernaturalist, secular-humanist paradigm. Those who share my wonder about the natural world may find these verses interesting, perhaps confirmatory, even transformative—I refer you to *Ode to Bertrand Russell,* below. Those who are content with a metaphysical faith that involves immaterial entities lying outside the objective universe (deities, afterlife, soul, spirits) may not wish to linger here. Or, you may dare to read boldly on, perhaps answering differently the questions that proved fatal to my adolescent faith.

LOVE, DEATH, HUMANISM

ODE TO BERTRAND RUSSELL
1872 - 1970

your words set me free
scales fell from wondering eyes,
correcting life's course

superstitions foiled,
country church's grip released,
dogma's chains broken

freethought flowed freely
in secular humanism's
sensible worldview

these sixty years on
I ponder the Universe
in your wise shadow

your book made me me,
enriched life beyond measure
—thank you, Lord Russell

Photo: Original copy of the book that changed my life in 1961 /150

I Tried

I read the bible,
I listened to Pastor Bob,
I pushed down my doubts

each Sunday morning
I sat still, as expected,
waiting for the light

Jews are confident
Catholics are sure they're right
Muslims too, I'm told

Mom said to trust God
I feared the torture of Hell
could I deserve that?

my young faith faltered,
I tried to make sense of it
—in the end, I failed

The abandoned church of my childhood, Knoxville, Missouri. Photo, revisited March 15, 2022 /241

LOVE, DEATH, HUMANISM

The Forbidden Question

this awkward schoolboy,
assigned to deep center field
by phys ed teacher

doubts had been brewing
about Sunday sermons' truths
on slippery slope:

Heaven and Hell, real?
why does prayer seem not to work?
and … (I dared not ask!)

trembling, knees wobbling,
that forbidden question burst:
and … does God exist?

fly ball came my way
frozen by fear, I dropped it
—I had reached the edge

The awkward, distracted boy /415

DAN DANA

How Do You Not Ask?

do you not wonder:
is your faith the correct one
of all the others?

how to reconcile
settled science with your faith,
since both can't be true?

does your life's work rest
on confidence that you're right
without crippling doubt?

since youth, I've scoured those
inescapable questions
—I could not NOT ask

not debating here,
I'm simply seeking to know,
how do you not ask?

Franciscan friar (London, 2023). His vows: "no money, no honey, no doubt" (poverty, chastity, faith) /392

LOVE, DEATH, HUMANISM

Humanists

we care for people
in their natural lifetimes,
we're good without gods

blind faith cannot see,
luring myths cloud our vision
of plain facts of life

inconvenient truth:
gods' will and heaven's bliss are
pre-science fake news

we're born, then we die,
relish this one awesome trip,
savor life's sweet scent

en route, please be kind,
love our fellow passengers
aboard this frail boat

Photo: loupiote /188

DAN DANA

Is Atheism a Faith?

is atheism
a belief system like those
we call religions?

if no evidence,
is not-believing belief?
or simply reason?

is end of living
your afterlife's beginning
if nothing happens?

can not-lifting-weights
be your daily exercise,
or just self-deceit?

I have a hobby:
not collecting foreign stamps,
saving precious time

/145

LOVE, DEATH, HUMANISM

First God

Sarasota sun
once brightened African eyes
and wondering minds

six million years past,
who first pondered mysteries:
what is it? who knows?

gives us light, warmth, time
—no science, yet, to know facts,
so we made stuff up

yearning for answers,
myths fed their hungry wonder,
hence "gods of the gap"*

now, we know stars' truth
but still worship Father Sun's
apocryphal sons

* The land between scientific knowledge and unexplained natural phenomena, where religions reside /55

Christian Cosmologists

that most odd creature,
the "Christian Cosmologist,"
should now be extinct

but specimens live,
defying laws of physics,
though sightings are rare

perhaps they possess
supernatural power
over Reason's rules?

I'm a stern skeptic
of my own cozy beliefs,
self-deception's tricks

as a scientist*
I ask, where's the evidence?
show me it's not myth

* I'm a curious hobbyist, not a practicing researcher. /367

LOVE, DEATH, HUMANISM

Pondering Infinity

"here" lies inbetween
multiverse and quantum world
on the cosmic scale

"now" spans time's range from
Big Bang to eternity
twixt unsure end-points

mind's eye is flummoxed,
infinity thwarts grasp of
limitless spacetime

as our inapt brain
collapses in sheer wonder
before Nature's scale,

we confront failure:
magical thinking invents
"SUPERnatural"

/87

DAN DANA

How Do I Love Thee?

God of all power,
Maker of the universe,
Knower of all things

Killer of children
by hunger, war, disease, hate,
where is Thy mercy?

Ally of fascists
who murder their enemies
who love other Gods

Denier of facts,
discoveries of science
that would disprove Thee

humans hath made Thee
of wishes and fantasies
—how can I love Thee?

Image by AI (ImageFX) /416

LOVE, DEATH, HUMANISM

Cosmic Boundaries

after end of time,
before beginning of time,
beyond edge of space

what's on other side?
Big Bang spawned this universe,
what was there before?

nonsense questions, these?
human scale lacks good answers,
need more dimensions?

"empty" space expands,
quantum scale's "spooky action,"
math sees what scopes can't

reality's bounds
surpass imagination,
science seeks to know

Photo by Hubble Space Telescope, NASA /71

DAN DANA

WHAT IS NOTHING?

does spacetime exist
if there is no "stuff" in it?
—I'm just wondering

if there is no "here"
where could "there" possibly be?
—no distance between

if there is no "now"
when could "then" possibly be?
—no future, no past

what might it "look" like
if no light illluminates,
there's no energy?

if every "thing" left,
if the Universe went blank,
what is left over?

These questions might appear frivolous, even silly. But "What is nothing?" is perhaps the most fundamental and perplexing question in cosmology.

Image: A metaphorical depiction (i.e., "something") of "nothing" /359

LOVE, DEATH, HUMANISM

Why Does Anything Exist?

how come existence?
the ultimate mystery
yet, we're here to ask

something from nothing?
why not just void empty space?
or not even that?

if god, then whence god?
prescience mystics conjured
some <u>super</u>nature

whence mathematics?
universe without numbers,
with nothing to count?

these vexing questions
are unanswerable, yet
I seem to exist!

/295

The Ultimate Question

why is there something,
existence of anything,
rather than nothing?

not the universe,
no empty space, no forces,
no gravitation

no laws of physics,
no spacetime, no quantum fields,
no mathematics

not even first cause,
nothing supernatural,
no one to know why

does this break your brain?
if not, perhaps you need to
repeat the question

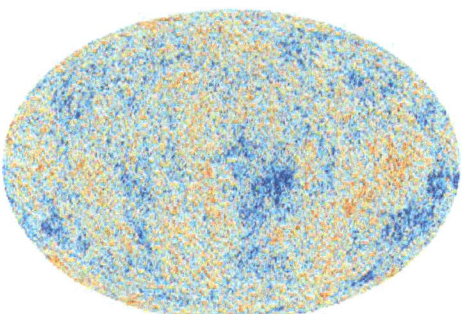

Image: ESA Planck satellite showing the cosmic microwave background
(relic light from the Big Bang) /15

LOVE, DEATH, HUMANISM

We Are Accidental People

some million years past,
our concestor's mom conceived,
one sperm got there first

bested his brothers,
every human since descends
—but what if other?

what history then?
whole other population,
wars, leaders, prophets

that quirk's chance result:
what is now would not have been,
same earth, other peeps

if other sperm won,
I would not be writing this,
nor you reading it

Image: Houston Museum of Natural Science. Our grandmother (10,000 generations ago). Fossil reconstruction from likely period of the most recent common ancestor (concestor) of all humans today. /74

DAN DANA

I Am African (and You Are Too)

Swahili greeting:
Sisi ni watoto wa
*Afrika … jambo!**

ancestors left home
five thousand lifespans ago,
adventuring north

inching around globe,
caves sheltered us from peril,
cold, carnivores, death

Euro-myth debunked:
invasive species is us,
natives oust natives

our bloodlines alloy,
we're all family, my friend
—African cousins

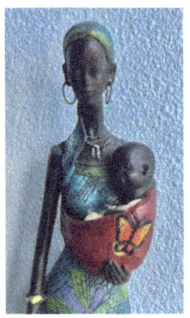

* Translation: "We are all children of Africa … hey!"
Photo of personal art (Susan is a mom-baby nurse.)   /108

LOVE, DEATH, HUMANISM

My Nigerian Atheist Friend

half a world away
near-neighbors in cyberspace
he must hide his truth

wife, friends, family
die-hard zealots of dogma
religionists all

God's set men seek wealth
streets littered with loud churches
monstrous billboards shout

so many pastors
shrilling mindboggling song-sprees
launch zombie-like trance

African dark zone
be careful, my new-found friend
your words give me hope

Most words and phrases above are lifted from his emails to me. He's the poet; I am his haiku arranger. Image is a generic silhouette, not his likeness. He must remain anonymous for his safety from violent religious zealots and theocratic government. Image by AI (ImageFX) /41

A Neanderthal Day

this cave has sheltered
our clan since the Beginning,
and will Evermore

our stone and bone tools,
made by elders of elders,
are kept in their place

our cooking hearth warms
sleeping beds of grass and ash
under auroch skins

spear points are sharpened,
we will hunt cave lion soon,
my son is learning

my hand with ochre
I made wall painting today
—sons' sons will know me

This typical day was replicated for 15,000 generations spanning 300,000 years until Neanderthal DNA became fully subsumed within Homo sapiens' genome by interbreeding about 40,000 years ago. They were our direct ancestors. Modern monotheistic religions emerged only about 2000 years ago. Photo: Krapina Cave Museum diorama, Croatia /417

LOVE, DEATH, HUMANISM

LIFE

life is natural
chemistry of universe,
Earth is not unique

four billion years on,
evolution continues,
we're not its endpoint

Goldilocks zones* teem,
Drake Equation** calculates
trillions of wet worlds

Rover may perform
autopsy of ancient life,
Mars' first coroner

exploring whether
life can find bio-niches,
if we're not alone

* Distance from a star where liquid water can exist on planet's surface
** The Drake Equation variants estimate the number of life-forms throughout the knowable universe

Selfie by Perseverance Rover on Mars (NASA, 2020) /126

DAN DANA

Be Here Now

I let myself Be,
watching my mind watch itself
with no greater goal

in my place in space,
a perch in the universe,
let myself be Here

this moment is real,
future's not yet, past is spent,
let myself be Now

don't push the river,
it will flow all by itself,
I'm only flotsam

I don't helm this boat,
a passenger on life's trip,
along for the ride

/181

LOVE, DEATH, HUMANISM

Celebrating Darwin Day: February 12

Covid's on the hunt,
evolution's not done yet,
hide behind your mask

nature's famous law:
"survival of the fittest"
—stay healthy, humans!

our tasty bits tempt
hungry predator to binge,
she can't eat just one

wily genes mutate,
natural selection works,
Darwin showed us how

seek gods' protection?
or gain knowledge through science?
nothing fails like prayer

Charles Darwin, born 12 February 1809, photo 1877 /180

DAN DANA

Happy Festivus

hail, winter solstice!
northern earthlings' shortest day,
axis' greatest tilt

let us celebrate
our Neolithic forebears'
Sun God's next rebirth

Stonehenge pagans' rites
or Saturnalia's heirs
—pick a tradition:

Hanukkah, Christmas,
or mischievous Festivus*
for the rest of us

let's join together
as secular humanists,
be kind and have fun!

* A parody holiday celebration first broadcast on a *Seinfeld* episode December 18, 1997.
Image by AI (ImageFX) /393

EPILOGUE

THE RIGHT SIDE OF HISTORY

I want to be on
the right side of history
when it is written

my words live in print,
on offer to the wide world,
though seldom noticed:

- ✓ climate will kill us
- ✓ America's star will fall
- ✓ religion is myth

- ✓ no, life is NOT good
- ✓ only science leads to truth
- ✓ love is the answer

some years(?) left to write
'til I slip away, unseen,
my words remaining

/403

LEGACY

one hundred haiku,
gleanings from these eighty years
along life's pathway:

how to make love work,
to face death eyes wide open,
how and why we're here

one day I'll expire,
life's horizon shall be breached,
but words may live on

—love made and love earned,
death faced free of needless fear,
good deeds done for all—

in readers' lived lives
—to no greater legacy
could I dare aspire

ABOUT ME

I am retired from a career in psychology, mediation, and education. I have authored two books on conflict resolution, one on secular humanism, and a current series consisting mostly of haiku quintets (an original art form devised in retirement).

Born in 1945 in rural Missouri, life experiences include:

- Serving in the U.S. Army in Vietnam (noncombat) and Panama Canal Zone (1966-1968)
- Earning a PhD in counseling psychology (University of Missouri, 1977)
- Teaching at University of Hartford (Connecticut) for 26 years and guest-lecturing at educational institutions on six continents
- Founding in 1985 and growing Mediation Training Institute, an Internet-based educational enterprise acquired in 2013 by Eckerd College (St Petersburg, Florida) and currently operated there
- Being a candidate for the U.S. House of Representatives (1998)
- Living, working, or traveling in over 85 countries and seven continents

Susan and I live in Sarasota, Florida. I am the father of one and grandfather of two.

ACKNOWLEDGEMENTS

Who knows where poetry comes from?
Only I (admittedly with the aid of online thesauri) composed, edited, and diligently revised these verses, whose nuances arose from deep wells of experience and emotion that often were a discovery to myself. Yet, none would exist without the inspiration, support, and influence of people listed below. So, I'm not the only author of this book. With gratitude, I acknowledge:

- LWR Scribes, a writers group in Sarasota, Florida
- Humanists of Sarasota Bay
- Assorted friends—you know who you are
- My family of origin, living and dead
- Su, my daughter
- Seamus and Claribel, my grandchildren, whose very existence motivated and inspired these verses far more profoundly and complexly than they know, a fact I hope they will someday, in moments of quiet reflection, recognize
- Susan, my muse, my artist model, my cohabitee, my primary love-object, my best friend, my other half

OTHER BOOKS

Post-retirement:

- *The Reason Revolution: Atheism, Secular Humanism, and the Collapse of Religion*
- *Haiku Quintets*
- *Science and Secularism: Haiku Quintets and Other Musings*
- *A Life Mostly Lived: True Stories in 85 Syllables*
- *Diary of a Young Man, 1968-1969: Coming of Age at a Cultural Crossroads*
- *Songs of the Pandemic: World Haiku*
- *Common Ground: Haiku, Mediation, and Police Reform*
- *Resisting Trumpism: Haiku Quintets*

Pre-retirement

- *Managing Differences: How to Build Better Relationships at Work and Home* (MTI Publications), in multiple languages
- *Conflict Resolution: Mediation Tools for Everyday Worklife (McGraw-Hill)*, in multiple languages
- *Talk It Out: 4 Steps to Managing People Problems in Your Organization* (Kogan Page)

Made in United States
Orlando, FL
23 September 2024